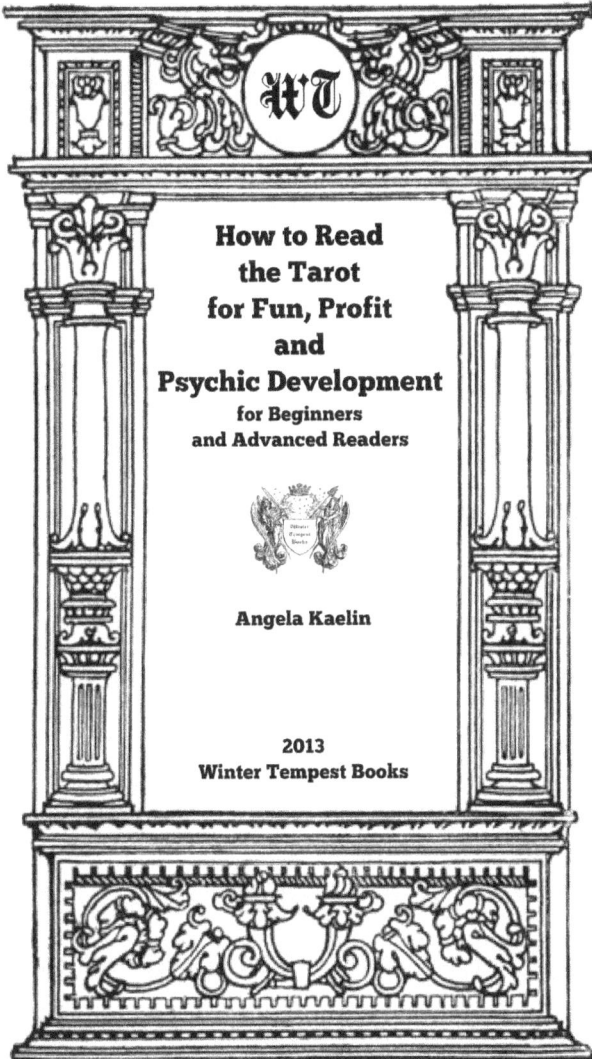

How to Read the Tarot for Fun, Profit and Psychic Development

for Beginners and Advanced Readers

Angela Kaelin

2013
Winter Tempest Books

ISBN: 0615823823
ISBN-13:978-0615823829
Winter Tempest Books

DEDICATION

In honor of my grandparents.

Contents

INTRODUCTION

There are many books that show tarot readers the basic meaning of the cards and how to arrange them, but few publications ever go beyond the mechanics of reading the tarot. Because you are unlikely to find such information in a tarot manual or anywhere else, I would like to share with you what I have learned in twenty-five years of professional tarot reading.

This little book takes you beyond the technical aspects of reading and describes what happens when you begin to read professionally for strangers. While tarot card reading is a practice unique to each individual, there are some common experiences shared by advanced readers. Often another level of psychic awakening comes with reading for others, in particular, reading for complete strangers for money.

Learning to read the tarot proficiently can benefit you socially, financially and intellectually. It is a pathway to developing greater psychic abilities.

Psychic ability is an ancient human trait. It is a higher one rather than a lower one; it is superhuman rather than animal. It is more than just intuition and truly a higher kind of extra-sensory ability. Just as your mind, by means of your physical eyes, can interpret signals in the ether and convert them into images, it can sense and interpret other signals and interpret them. In most of us, this is a forgotten ability, but not a lost one.

Throughout this book, two terms are used which may be unfamiliar to some people. The term "querent" refers to the person who comes to you with a question or your client. The term "tableau" is another word for the layout of the cards. These terms were in common usage among readers in the 1930s and 1940s.

The tarot cards are a lifelong study and represent a journey into a greater understanding of the world, both visible and invisible. As with any endeavor, we must begin at the beginning.

THE TRUTH ABOUT THE TAROT

No one knows the real origins of the tarot, however, researchers agree that there was once a card game played in Italy in the 15th century called "Tarocchi." This deck of cards was similar to tarot decks available today, with 22 major arcana cards and 56 minor arcana cards for a total of 78. While the cards were used as a game and for gambling, there is a great deal of tradition in the West surrounding their use for divination.

The oldest surviving tarot cards date to circa 1428-1447 and were commissioned by the Visconti family of Milan, Italy and attributed to the Italian fresco artist, Bonifacio Bembo. The art work reflects contemporary life in 15th century Milan, painted in rich colors and gilded. Some of the original cards from this deck are missing, so they have been reconstructed by various modern artists. Presently, numerous versions of the Visconti deck are available. The original Visconti tarot cards along with cards from other historical tarot decks reside in private art collections.

Whatever the tarot's original purpose was, it is apparent that its 22 major arcana very neatly correspond to the 22 paths of the Hebrew Qabala, a system of ancient knowledge which is, at least, 2,000 years old and quite possibly much older. The 56 minor arcana cards correspond with combinations of the four elements, the planets and their astrological houses.

It is highly unlikely that these correspondences are coincidental or an afterthought. They were clearly part of the original design, therefore, the designer must have been an initiate of the highest degree.

Why Read Tarot Cards?

If you are a beginner or have only thought that you might like to become a card reader, it is important to consider your reasons for wanting to do this. You can gain a lot by learning this skill and all of the following are good, valid motivations for learning to read tarot cards.

1. To become more popular. Tarot reading is a lot of fun for the person whose cards are being read. It makes people feel good to have the focus placed on themselves for the duration of a reading. This is why being a tarot reader can make you very popular. You will quickly become the center of attention at parties and you will be met with excited requests to "Read my cards!" You will likely meet many new people and possibly gain a wider circle of friends as a tarot reader. This is especially true if you become very proficient in this art because people will seek you out. This one reason, alone, is enough to make tarot reading a worthwhile endeavor.

2. To gain insight into the present and into the future possibilities of any given situation you encounter in life. This is clearly an advantage to you that can provide an edge in personal relationships and in business.

3. To solve problems. The tarot cards can provide creative solutions to problems by providing information and showing you possibilities that might not have been considered before. When you read the cards for yourself, they act like a sounding board. When you do not have a friend to consult or confide in, you can ask questions of the cards and they will suggest answers to you, which you might not have thought of entirely on your own. There is no better or quicker method for obtaining answers when there is a question of "What is really happening in this situation?" or "Should I take this opportunity or another?"

4. To expand your awareness. The tarot deck is a tool for enlightenment and personal growth. Learning to read tarot cards causes you to dwell more on matters of a spiritual nature and gives you a broader perspective on life.

5. To expand or enhance your psychic abilities or simply to become aware of them in the first

place. You will probably find your overall sensitivity becomes more finely tuned as a result of reading the cards. As you continue on your journey with the cards and, especially, as you become a professional tarot reader, other psychic abilities will begin to unfold.

6. To gain initiation into ancient mysteries, particularly in relation to astrology and the Qabala. The tarot cards are an instrument of true initiation when you make a serious study of them beyond the descriptions in your tarot manual.

7. To make a little money. If you live in an area where it is legal to read tarot cards in exchange for remuneration, fortune-telling may become a source of a little extra income for you. You have the opportunity to earn money by giving readings to individuals or entertaining at parties. This is something you can begin doing as soon as you become confident in your card reading.

Who Should Read the Cards?

Anyone who is attracted to the idea of reading tarot cards should definitely give it a try. The main trait a tarot reader needs to succeed is desire.

If your only desire is to become proficient enough to entertain your friends, meet new people, increase your popularity and make a little extra money, you will likely not find this a difficult goal to meet.

But, if you truly dedicate yourself to the study of the tarot cards, they can take you places, psychically, spiritually and physically, that you might never have imagined possible. This is because the tarot cards hold the key to ancient mysteries, once only known by the initiates of secret societies.

How is It Possible to Know the Future?

This question is not easy to answer. The only thing that seems completely obvious is that the world is not as we have been taught to believe it is.

At a fundamental level, this world – the five-sense reality we share – can be described as particles of atoms and waves. Particles are somewhere between physical matter and pure energy. Waves are directed energy. It is a vibrant, ever-changing energy that comprises the most seemingly solid objects. For this reason, nothing around us is entirely fixed. This fact makes the art of predicting the future a challenging one because we cannot know exactly what will happen, but we can foretell what might happen or what is likely to occur under the right conditions.

Future events involve a mutable combination of factors, which are either inside or outside of the querent's control. A tarot reader may be likened to a person observing an intersection from the vantage point of a high building above. The observer may be able to see that two cars are about to collide, if they continue on the same course. But, if one of the drivers changes his course at the last minute, the collision may be averted.

A psychic forecaster can tell what will happen, if all the factors involved in the situation remain the same; if everyone involved stays on their present course, then, certain events or circumstances are likely to result. But, if the people involved change something before the event comes to pass, the outcome may be different. A skilled tarot reader is able to tell a querent about circumstances he or she may not yet be aware of, which they can use to steer onto a safer path and veer away from danger.

So, not everything about the future can be known because of the element of free will. But, circumstances, possibilities and likelihoods can be determined.

2

HOW TO SELECT A TAROT DECK

Some people believe that a tarot deck can only be acquired as a gift, however, this is only superstition. You do not have to wait for someone else to buy a deck of cards for you. You can purchase your own.

Furthermore, there is nothing wrong with acquiring a used deck that is in good condition. In fact, some tarot enthusiasts collect vintage decks. The real power to read the cards resides within you, not the deck of cards. They are only a tool and the information you receive during a reading does not come from them; it comes from both yourself and the querent.

Not only is it unnecessary to wait for someone to give you a deck, the cards may have more meaning to you when you choose them yourself. Here are some helpful guidelines for selecting a first deck:

Choose an actual tarot deck of 78 cards instead of an oracle deck. Oracle decks are fine. In fact, many of them are very good and you can obtain accurate readings with them, but they are not the same as tarot decks, which have a major and minor arcana.

Choose a deck that can be read with the cards in reverse. Occasionally, you will find tarot decks, especially the medieval classics, in which the cards are identical whether placed upright or reversed. Some tarot readers do not read in the reverse, however, doing so adds another dimension to your readings. The reversal of a card in a tableau can change its meaning altogether or mitigate its influence in the reading.

Above all, choose a tarot deck that you are attracted to and feel comfortable using. Any deck that speaks to you can be a good one and working with a variety of different ones can help you expand your skills.

The Best Tarot Decks

Overall, the A.E. Waite deck may be the best one for beginning readers, although it has some imperfections. There are numerous variations on this deck, in fact, most modern decks were inspired by the Waite deck, which was the first to illustrate the meanings of the cards. The Quick and Easy Tarot, The Universal Waite, The Herbal Tarot and the standard Rider-Waite are examples of good beginner decks.

If you are still in the early stages of learning to read the tarot and do not like having to consult your tarot manual, then you might especially enjoy The Quick and Easy Tarot, which has the meanings of the cards, both upright and reversed, printed on the face of each one. This can certainly make things easier for the absolute beginner.

It is good to become familiar with any of the Waite decks. They are glamorous enough, yet do not feature imagery that is too dark or distasteful to the uninitiated. If you can master the Waite deck, then you can easily use any other tarot deck.

A tarot template is, also, useful for beginners. This is a large piece of paper with a diagram of a tableau, like the popular Celtic Cross, printed on it. It shows the beginning reader exactly where to lay the cards and the meaning of each card in a particular position in the tableau. Some beginner decks come with a template. But, it is better if you create your own by consulting the information about lay-outs in your tarot deck's instruction booklet. The act of creating the template will impress the meaning of each of the card positions on your memory. Soon, you will no longer require a template.

When you are divining for another person, the cards provide a focal point for both the reader and the querent. For the querent, the cards hold a mystical fascination. For the reader, they may trigger psychic images, sounds and other experiences regarded as paranormal. It is true that genuine psychics can perform readings without cards, however, it simply would not be the same experience without the esoteric beauty and mystery of the tarot cards.

While you can give good readings with any deck you choose, Crowley's *Thoth* deck is the very best for performing very precise readings. It is similar to the Waite deck, but the cards contain a great deal more hidden imagery and symbolism that prompts psychic insights, especially for those who have made a study of astrology and the Qabala.

Care of the Cards

Tarot decks are not inexpensive, so it is important to care for your deck. Do not allow the cards to become bent and protect the waxed surface for smooth shuffling. Some people are very particular to the point of superstition about how their cards are stored and who touches them.

Here are a few common sense rules for keeping your decks safe and in good shape:

1. Only handle the cards with clean, dry hands.

2. Do not eat or drink while handling the cards.

3. Lay them on a clean surface. You may use a special tarot cloth, a scarf, tablecloth or altar cloth.

4. Handle the cards carefully to avoid bending them.

5. Store them in a bag or wooden tarot box.

Shuffling normal sized tarot cards takes a little practice. Smaller sized cards are available for readers who have difficulty getting their hands around a standard-sized deck.

Decide how much you want to let other people touch your cards. Some tarot readers believe that having the querent touch the cards transmits the person's energy to them; they feel that there is an element of psychometry involved in tarot reading. Many readers simply like to make their clients feel more involved in the process by allowing them to shuffle the cards or, at least, to cut the cards before a reading.

Allowing querents to shuffle the cards can sometimes become a hindrance to a successful reading in the form of an awkward distraction, if the person is not comfortable handling cards. Therefore, you may want to limit your querent's involvement to simply cutting the deck once before you lay them out.

Another problem with letting other people handle your cards is that they can quickly become soiled and bent. This can affect their functionality and shorten the life of your deck. If the surface of your cards becomes sticky from mishandling, you may use Goo Gone or a similar de-greasing product to clean them. Do not apply the product directly to the card; only apply a couple of drops to a soft, clean cloth or disposable towel and wipe the surface of the card lightly and gently.

The truth is that you can perform accurate readings without anyone else ever touching your cards.

3

HOW TO PREPARE FOR TAROT READINGS

Total preparation for reading the tarot cards begins long before you have an appointment scheduled. It involves maintaining a healthy, emotionally balanced life style. This means taking special care of both your physical health and emotional well-being by eating well and staying on an even keel by avoiding drama and practicing a little simple meditation.

A commonly overlooked component to making a successful psychic connection is diet. Avoid the consumption of alcoholic beverages, especially before or during a reading. Also, avoid the use mind-altering drugs. Along with the avoidance of drugs and alcohol, many occultists are, also, vegetarians because avoiding meat in favor of raw foods and vegetables alters your vibratory rate and enhances psychic abilities. If you do not choose an alcohol-free, vegetarian life style, at least, limit your consumption of alcohol and red meat prior to performing tarot readings.

Many psychics avoid heavy meals right before a session. Avoiding red meat and nuts for a few days in favor of raw vegetables can produce a profoundly positive effect on your psychic abilities. Fresh carrot and parsley juice helps facilitate second sight. Minerals like chromium and selenium nourish the nervous system and facilitate psychic abilities. Consuming a small amount of fish and Omega 3 and Omega 6 Fatty Acids can, also, enhance your psychic abilities.

The famous French astrologer, apothecary and prophet, Nostradamus credited Bing cherries with enhancing his own psychic abilities; he was known to make cherry preserves for which he gives a recipe in his first published work, entitled, *EXCELLENT & USEFUL Treatise to all Needed Who Want Knowledge of Several Exquisite Recipes ... Newly Composed by Master Michel de Nostredame, Doctor of Medicine in the City of Salon de Craux en Provence*, published in 1555. Nostradamus ate a small amount of this jelly every day to maintain his ability to forecast the future.

A recipe for cherry jelly based on his instructions may be found in the Appendix along with a comprehensive list of herbs, foods, vitamins and minerals necessary for the optimal functioning of your sixth senses.

Conversely, if your psychic abilities begin to

open up too fast and you feel that you are "seeing too much" and want to turn down or shut off this ability temporarily, treat yourself to a hamburger or a steak. This seems to have a grounding effect for psychics. This is why many occultists, at least, experiment with vegetarianism. You can learn to control your psychic abilities by means of adjusting your diet.

Mental Focus and Concentration

Along with certain herbs and foods, the regular practice of any kind of meditation, breath training, yoga or self-hypnosis can help you to become calm and more able to fine tune your psychic abilities.

As a regular practice, inhaling to the count of 11 and exhaling to the count of 7 (hold for the count of 3 upon inhale and exhale) for 15 cycles at each session will increase your psychic energy supply. This simple discipline will help provide you with some mental training to keep focused on your tarot readings. If you can train your mind to focus for short periods of time, you can train it to focus for longer ones. Once you've mastered this breathing exercise for 15 cycles, expand it to 20, then 25 and so on. Practice it while you are relaxing on the sofa, enjoying a warm bath or falling asleep at night.

As you sit across from the person for whom you intend to read, put aside all joking and idle chitchat. Announce to the querent what you are about to do, for example, say, "I am now going to go into a light trance as I take a few deep breaths and then we will begin the reading." Take two or three deep breaths as you focus on detaching yourself from your own mundane cares and thoughts. When you feel that you have mentally latched onto the energy of your querent, then you are ready to begin.

If you are proficient at handling the cards, shuffling them can be an excellent way to relax because it is a rhythmic activity that both busies the hands and frees the mind. If you are not good at shuffling, simply practice, practice, practice. Tarot readers must be able to handle the cards smoothly.

Understanding hypnotic anchoring is particularly useful to tarot readers. You can condition your own mind to quickly go into trance by, for example, wrapping a pen on the table twice or viewing a particular object for a few seconds. Or, you may devise a phrase that you use, silently, to signal to your subconscious to instantly go into the proper meditative state.

The signal you devise is an anchor that prompts your subconscious mind to immediately go into a trance. Let us suppose you have chosen to gaze at a black gemstone for a few seconds in order to signal your subconscious mind. Create the anchor by saying to yourself, "Whenever I gaze at this black gemstone, I will immediately go into a trance." Then, keep that object where you can see it whenever you perform readings.

Simply thinking, "I want to perform an accurate and helpful reading for this person," can become an anchor that takes your mental energy in the direction it needs to go. Depending on your individual preferences, you might benefit from invoking the power of a deity, helpful entity or your own higher power to assist you in what you are about to do.

To prepare for a reading, do whatever it takes to get yourself relaxed and focused on the matter at hand. Eventually, you should be able to condition yourself to go into a meditative state very quickly by shuffling the cards and taking a couple of deep breaths, staring at something black or by means of some anchoring device of your own invention. As you proceed, you will find what works best for you.

Once you feel that you are calmly focused on your purpose, ask the querent to formulate his or her question, either silently or aloud. Once that is done, you can begin the process of laying out the cards and reading them.

Preparing a Place to Read

First and foremost, choose a clean, calm, quiet place in which to conduct your reading. Performing your tarot readings in the same place each time can help condition your mind to go into the proper meditative state.

It is important for you to be in good physical and emotional condition. Even if you are a very practiced reader, you will find that it is difficult to read during times of turmoil in your personal life. Try to keep your own life on a relaxed and emotionally calm course as much as possible. Try to avoid doing readings at times when you are physically ill, emotionally upset or otherwise distracted. Avoid upsetting people and situations, as much as possible.

If there has been any sort of arguing, fighting or any other emotionally upsetting activity in a place, it can leave a palpable residue, which seems to linger in the air. The best thing to do is find somewhere else to read. If that is not possible, cleanse the location of these energies before you begin your reading.

There are lots of ways to get the job done, so just choose the one that is most comfortable for you. For instance, a Wiccan might cast a circle of protection to block out any energetic interference during the reading. Negative energy in a room or an entire house can be driven out by smudging with a White Sage bundle, followed by smudging with a braid of sweet grass. These items are available from most metaphysical stores.

An emotionally upset person can also be smudged before a reading by a similar method. Simply, light the sage bundle and allow the smoke to drift around the person or the area to be cleansed. Follow this with a similar procedure using the sweet grass.

Also, you can order negative energies to depart in the name of Jesus Christ, which can be remarkably effective without regard to any religious or other beliefs.

Again, if it works, do it and do whatever works best for you.

HOW TO PERFORM A SUCCESSFUL READING

Shuffling and Laying the Cards

The shuffling and laying of the cards is the most important part of a reading because this is when you bridge the connection between the querent and the spirit world.

Decide what sort of card shuffling and cutting ritual you want to use. Instructions in some books on the subject are very specific about how many times to cut the cards even specifying which hand to use, however, you can perform readings very effectively with or without these little ceremonies.

My own method is to go into a light trance state, then shuffle the cards until I feel that I have tuned myself into the querent, which is much like mentally finding a particular station with a radio dial. It is an interesting phenomenon in tarot card reading that as you are shuffling the cards there will be a point when you will have the urge to stop. You could go on shuffling, but it doesn't seem right. The moment I have the urge to stop, I do. Then, I cut the cards once and begin laying them face up one at a time without the querent ever touching them. It is plain and simple but it works as well as any elaborate ritual.

Deal the cards out in the order in which you intend to read them. Place any cards not used in the tableau face down on the table.

When you are reading the cards in their reversed positions, look at them from your own perspective and not that of the querent.

As a beginner, you may refer to the basic meanings given in the instruction booklet that comes with your deck. For each card, certain meanings will have more relevance in a given position. Keep in mind that cards can have very different meanings from one reading to another.

To advance as a reader, you must make a study of the cards that goes beyond the scope of any instruction booklet or tarot manual. Approach tarot reading as a science, first. Then, apply your intuition to this science. As you advance, the significance of certain symbols will seem to leap off the cards at you. You might get pictures or words in your head that seem to come out of thin air; you will not recognize them as your own thoughts, which is how you know it is coming from some other source. When this happens, simply acknowledge it and allow it to flow through naturally.

In the beginning of your endeavors, you may find it helpful to keep a journal of your readings. In this journal you may note the cards that come up in a given reading and what they mean to you in this particular instance, however, it may be even more useful to record the outcome of the readings you give, so that you can check your accuracy in predicting the outcome of future events.

Ethics

Frequently, someone you are reading for will have a question about someone else. They may be worried that their spouse is cheating, that their child is in trouble or they may want to find out what is in the mind of an opponent in a legal matter. There are some readers who feel it is immoral and an invasion of privacy to read the cards for someone who has not given his or her consent.

If you believe it is immoral, then do not do it. For those who do not feel guilty about doing such readings, here is some advice on how to do it:

Find the face card that best represents the person for whom you intend to read in absentia. To find this card, go through the deck with the cards face up until one of the court cards stands out to you. If you are a more psychically advanced reader, you may get an image of the person in your mind, in which case you should locate the court card in the deck that most closely resembles this person.

Then, describe your impressions to the client and

ask them if this sounds like the person. If the client says, "Yes," then you can be pretty sure you've got a psychic fix on the person in question. Place the card face up as the first one in the tableau and then continue dealing the cards out. Finish the reading as you would any other.

By this method, it is possible to see what is going on in a person's household, with their spouse or someone else and where the situation is likely to lead without intervention. Be honest with the querent about what you see.

Whether or not you regard the ability to see into someone else's private affairs as an invasion of privacy, you will find that as your psychic abilities develop you will do this spontaneously and sometimes unintentionally. Also, consider that every person has the ability to psychically block information about themselves and to erect psychic barriers either consciously or subconsciously.

Therefore, it is really not something you should feel guilty about, nor should you allow others to make you feel guilty about having this natural ability.

Many times, querents will become emotional during readings because you are bringing up events that are highly personal to them, sometimes these are things they have never told anyone about. Always be sensitive to your clients feelings and keep a box of tissues handy. This is, also, why readings are best done in complete privacy.

Some readers always try to put a positive spin on what they see and always give upbeat readings, however, if you have information that can help the querent and you do not reveal it for fear of appearing negative, you are doing your client a disservice. Always try to give true and honest readings, so that your client can make his or her own decisions about a matter with more clarity.

As a tarot reader and incidental spiritual counselor, you are morally obligated not to discuss your clients' private affairs with other people. You should have as much discretion in these matters as a priest and keep your clients' confidence.

If the Cards Fail You

Even if you are highly skilled tarot reader and psychic, sometimes tarot readings can still go awry. Keep in mind that the most common questions people have revolve around relationships and money. They are worried about their jobs, their businesses, their children, their spouses or finding love. Most people are very materialistic and focused on the short-term rather than the long-term.

It is a common practice among some tarot readers to begin a reading by asking for the client's birth date. It is a good idea for beginning readers who have a basic feel for astrological sun signs to use this little crutch. It is not 100% accurate, but it can sometimes give you an edge if you are nervous about your psychic abilities or get stumped during the course of a tarot reading. The modern classic, *Linda Goodman's Love Signs*, is still an excellent book from which to learn the basic characteristics of astrological sun signs.

If you find a reading is not going well,

sometimes it is because the client is mentally scattered. Most definitely, if the querent has been drinking alcohol, is mentally ill or if he or she is on medication, you will have difficulty achieving an easy psychic rapport with them.

If you are faced with a particularly difficult, drunken or disturbed client, once you recognize their condition, try to politely excuse yourself. Tell them you are unable to do the reading at this time (because you have a headache, you are ill, etc.) and ask them to come back another day.

It is always better not to read for such people, but if you are a professional reader, you may not always be in a good position to decline, for example, if you are reading at a party or you have been hired by an entertainment agency. Because of the lack of rapport, you may have to approach the reading as if the client were a third party and do the reading as you would for someone in absentia.

Occasionally, you will get a hard-core skeptic or someone who wants to test your abilities. This is usually not a problem as long as the querent is not lying to purposely mislead you or psychically blocking you. To determine if they are blocking you, observe their posture. If they have their arms crossed in a defiant manner, politely ask them to place their hands on the reading table palms up. You will usually find that the reading goes much easier after that. Most people who block you are not doing it intentionally.

If you still feel that you are being blocked or if the person is very unable to focus on their question, you may still have trouble making the psychic connection. Again, try reading as if the person is in absentia. If this fails, you may have to resort to astrology or some other method of divination to answer specific questions satisfactorily.

If you are reading for a particularly difficult person in exchange for money, it is better not to argue with them and just refund their money and send them on their way.

I once had a client who came in with her husband. I read for her in private, but her husband was not far away, so I had to speak in a low voice because it was apparent from the reading that she was involved in affairs with more than one older man and that these affairs involved gifts and monetary gain. But, as I was doing the reading the woman's eyes grew larger and she repeatedly shook her head and said, "No." She insisted that I was completely wrong and since I was apparently unable to properly read for her, I refunded her money.

A few weeks later another woman came to me and said that her friend had come for a reading, but I was unable to read for her. I remembered the first woman and the reading distinctly because, at the time, I was so sure I was right, despite her vehement denials. I do not usually share information about a reading with anyone, but since she said I was wrong, I told her what the reading seemed to reveal. This woman told me that it was all true. The woman I had read for was, in fact, engaged in multiple affairs with older men for monetary gain, but she was so terrified by the accuracy of my reading that she completely denied the whole thing.

Sometimes people who do not believe in psychics will ask you to read for them merely out of idle curiosity or on a lark. Usually, reading for such people is not a problem. But, there are those who are skeptics out of fear that there may actually be something to E.S.P. The idea of a stranger being able to peer into their lives is very frightening to them, especially if they have secrets, however, most people you read for will find your psychic abilities very reassuring.

As you become a more practiced reader, you will learn when you are "in the zone." You will simply know when you are right.

Even if you are a less than perfect card reader, it is important to be aware of other people's feelings in delicate matters and always try to help them. Many people go to tarot readers only during times of trouble in their lives. So, always handle your clients with care. If you do, they are more likely to return to you and recommend you to their friends.

Psychic Hygiene

Occasionally, you may find that you feel very strange after a reading for someone, particularly if the querent is experiencing mental or emotional disturbances. This may be because you have allowed your energy fields to merge with theirs and now you are retaining some of their disturbed energy in your own bioenergetic field.

Sometimes you are immediately aware that you are retaining thoughts and emotions that are not your own. At other times, you may not notice it until later in the evening when you are winding down.

You can remove this energy by visualizing the etheric cords that are still connecting you to the querent and then imagine cutting them with a large pair of scissors.

You can, also, dissolve this residual energy in your auric field by bathing in sea salt and four or five drops of lavender oil. Once should be sufficient, but, if later you still feel disturbed or experience thoughts or emotions that do not seem to be your own, cleanse your aura again.

HOW TO READ THE TAROT

HOW TO START READING THE TAROT
FOR MONEY

A tarot reader performs a service and is entitled to remuneration. You do not have to be highly skilled to perform tarot readings for entertainment purposes and beginning to read for fair compensation is mostly a matter of having enough confidence to do it. As a beginner, you can become steadily more proficient at giving readings simply practicing on yourself, friends and family using only the cards and the little instruction booklets that are provided with each deck.

A book, entitled *Professional Tarot: The Business of Reading, Consulting and Teaching* by Christine Jette, provides specific information about setting up a tarot reading business. But, for most readers, it is not necessary to go as far as creating a business entity and getting a business license unless you plan to open a brick and mortar shop where your primary service is tarot reading.

Try to be aware of the laws in any city or jurisdiction in which you plan to read the tarot. There are many places in the United States where immoral and un-Constitutional laws and ordinances against psychic readings or fortune-telling exist, although they are rarely enforced. But, they have been used to shut down metaphysical bookstores and discourage psychics from performing readings. According to news reports, raids on metaphysical bookstores and arrests of psychics are usually prompted by a complaint.

For example, in 1991 in Independence, Missouri, undercover police conducted a sting operation over the course of five months before raiding a metaphysical bookstore. Between 1991 and 1992, police perpetrated a spate of such raids on tarot readers in Missouri, Connecticut and Pennsylvania, who were receiving donations of as little as $10.00 per reading.[1, 2, 3]

There have, also, been instances where tarot readers were accused of making a medical diagnosis without a license to practice medicine.

Even if you take the work you do very seriously, it is a good idea to describe your services as "entertainment." In fact, it is a form of entertainment. Frequently, you will see readers stating that their services are "for entertainment purposes only." This is not a bad idea from a legal standpoint and it is something you can point to in the event that someone acts on your advice with negative results or tries to accuse you of doing something illegal.

When you set out to investigate the laws in your area, do it carefully. Try not to attract too much attention to yourself. If you call a government office to inquire about a law, you do not have to identify yourself by name, so simply state your question. Frequently, the people at the office you call will seem baffled by your questions and will not have an answer for you, anyway. Sometimes, the best thing you can do to avoid trouble with government officials or religious fanatics is to simply stay off their radar.

As a precaution, some tarot readers acquire ministerial licenses and ordinations from organizations like Universal Life Church (www.ulc.net) in Modesto, California. While these are not invalid, they are not particular necessary, either. But, it costs next to nothing if it makes you feel better to say that you are an ordained, licensed minister. Although, the license means nothing in many, if not most, states.

Psychics and tarot readers in the U.K. have been largely protected by the 1951 Fraudulent Mediums Act, under which prosecutors have the difficulty of proving fraud and dishonest intent in order to secure a conviction. Prosecutions have been rare since its passage, but the law has been threatened by the country's association with the European Union.

The fact is that tarot readers are still persecuted in many places. Therefore, you should always be mindful of the laws and ordinances in a particular place and be careful not to make statements that could be construed as medical or legal advice whenever possible. Although, if corrupt law enforcement agents are determined to arrest you on a trumped up charge, they will and it will not matter if you have any kind of special license or not. Unfortunately, some things have changed very little since the Middle Ages.

Opportunities for Tarot Readers

In this day and age, you do not have to have a brick and mortar business to be a tarot reader; it is easy to put up a web site devoted to your tarot reading. Print some business cards, design a brochure, acquire a costume and advertise yourself to read at parties. Contact local entertainment agencies and event planners and let them know you are available. You can, also, offer readings over the phone using PayPal or a similar online payment processor.

If you feel comfortable with the idea and you have a good place to do it, you can invite people to your home for readings. Or, you can go to their homes.

Many metaphysical stores, especially in larger cities, have in-house card readers. If you are in the right place, you can make a decent living just doing readings for patrons without having your own shop.

Psychic fairs, Renaissance Fairs and paranormal conferences all present opportunities for the professional tarot reader. Usually, all you need is a little card table or tray, a small cloth and a couple of fold-up chairs. Do a little research for conferences and fairs coming up in your area, contact the organizers and ask them how much it costs to set up as a vendor.

When you accept payment from your clients, describe it as a "donation." This has become customary among tarot readers and it is done in an attempt to avoid being accused of doing something illegal. Depending on the cost of living where you are, you might suggest a donation of anywhere from $20.00 to $80.00 for a session. Determine your donation amount based on what the market will bear.

If you are conducting parties, you should be fairly compensated for your time, your skills and the cost of travel. You will have to handle a lot of readings in a row, which can be draining. You may, also, want to bring personal security or an assistant with you. Investigate the rates of other entertainers in your area and determine your rates, accordingly. Most tarot readers charge a larger amount for the first hour to cover the costs of travel and a lower amount for each hour after that.

Be creative when marketing your services. Let people know what you do. Always keep your tarot cards with you in case you have the unexpected opportunity to read for someone.

6

HOW TO PERFORM PHENOMENALLY PRECISE READINGS

If you want to go deeper, beyond reading simply to entertain, consulting tarot manuals when you cannot remember basic card meanings or relying only on intuition, then you must delve into the occult science that is the apparent basis for the tarot.

Aleister Crowley's *Thoth* deck is the one that can help you probe deeper into the mysteries of the tarot and enable you to give the most precise readings. Of course, it is possible to perform adequate readings with this or any other deck without devoting long periods of time to study, but if you want to be the best reader you can be, really improve the quality and precision of your readings and expand your psychic abilities, the *Thoth* deck is the best one. It provides very explicit and accurate representations of symbols from the Qabala, the elements, the planets and astrological houses right on each card of the deck. Aleister Crowley broke his oath to reveal the esoteric secrets in the *Thoth* deck.

How to Study the Major Arcana

To fully understand the major arcana, it is necessary to study the letters of the Hebrew alphabet and the corresponding paths of the Qabala. In the course of this study, you may want to set up an index card file with each letter, its Qabalistic path, general meanings and the corresponding tarot card and teach yourself by the flash card method. An excellent book to use in this study is Israel Regardie's *A Garden of Pomegranates*. Couple it with a study of Crowley's own manual for this deck, entitled *The Book of Thoth*, which, unlike modern tarot manuals, goes into great detail about the symbolism he used in the design of this deck. Also, recommended are Dion Fortune's *The Mystical Qabala*, and Aleister Crowley's *Liber 777*, both of which are available in the public domain.

How you construct your index card file is an individual matter. The example below shows you how I constructed mine for the major arcana beginning with "alpha," the first letter of the Hebrew alphabet. I placed each one of the 22 Hebrew letters on the front side of a heavy index card and the name of the symbol, its meaning, its path on the Qabalistic Tree of Life and other pertinent meanings and associations on the back side.

On the front of the index card, place the symbol for the Hebrew letter, Aleph:

א

On the reverse side of the index card, write out the name of the letter along with other important associations:

Aleph, which means ox; Path No. 11, joining Keser to Chokmah; Air. Aleph is associated with the eagle and Jupiter; the dove featured on the tarot card is associated with Isis or Mary. This is the card of the Fool; its number is zero. Other associations: Dionysus; the Green Man; springtime; emptiness; silliness; foolishness; the April Fool; alpha, the beginning.

When determining what information to include on the back side of your index card, consider that the most important aspects of the major arcana revolve around the paths of the Qabala, the seven planets, the four elements and the signs of the Zodiac. Include any other details that stand out or seem significant to you as you observe the symbolism of each tarot card and read the associations in The Garden of Pomegranates or in Crowley's own manual for this deck, The Book of *Thoth*.

Memorize the information you have written on these index cards. The mere act of researching these symbols, their meanings and associations and writing them down will help you remember them. Keep them as a reference and study them until you are able to look at each one of the major arcana cards and give a comprehensive description of each symbol and what it means to you both academically and personally.

How to Study the Minor Arcana

The cards of the minor arcana are divided into two types: Court cards and numbered cards. They are divided into the four suits: Wands; cups; swords and discs. Wands represent the fire element; cups represent the water element; swords represent the air element and discs represent the earth element.

With the exception of the aces, each of the numbered cards shows the symbols for a planet and an astrological house. Most numbered cards, also, have a corresponding Sephiroth from the Qabalah, but this is of secondary importance to the planets in their houses and the other symbolism on the cards. Each of the aces represents the pure root of its particular element.

Familiarity with the astrological symbols for the planets, the signs of the zodiac and their basic meanings is fundamental to your study of the minor arcana. The Astrologer's Handbook by Sakoian and Acker is an excellent reference for studying the influence of the planets in the astrological houses.

Make a complete study of each of the planets and the astrological signs. You should be familiar with the symbols for each planet and zodiac sign, which are hidden in the artwork the minor arcana cards from 2 to 10. To create an index card file for the minor arcana, place a planetary or astrological symbol on the front side of an index card and its name, associations and meanings on the back side.

Study the influence of the planets in each house of the zodiac, which will give you a basic overview of the occult science of astrology. This system of planets influencing houses is fairly simple once you know the names, symbols and meanings for each planet and zodiac sign.

Only after you have completely mastered this, study the ten Sephiroth of the Qabala by the same method.

Court cards can represent either a real person or a situation. Understanding the court cards along with their elemental and Qabalisitic correlations can make their interpretation much easier and more illuminating.

The court cards represent the elements which correspond with the four letters of the Tetragrammaton: Yod; Heh; Vau and Heh. In order, they are the Knights, Queens, Princes and Princesses and respectively they correspond to the elements as follows: Fire; water; air and earth.

The correspondences of the court cards are easy to recall if you memorize the following:

Knights = Fire
Queens = Water
Princes = Air
Princesses = Earth

Wands = Fire
Cups = Water
Swords = Air
Discs = Earth

Upon examining the court cards you will see this combination of elements represented. For example, the Knight of Discs represents the fiery aspect of earth because knights correspond with fire and discs correspond with earth.

Meditating on individual cards of the *Thoth* deck can lead to "A-ha" moments as you draw connections. Aleister Crowley's own expanded manual for the *Thoth* deck, entitled, *The Book of Thoth*, is the only tarot manual that will really provide you any deep insights into the meaning of the tarot cards. But it is difficult to fully understand without making the preliminary study of the aforementioned subjects and Crowley urges you to meditate on the information he provides, as well.

An entire lifetime could be spent studying the meanings of the tarot cards and mysteries would still remain. Learning to read the tarot well is so beneficial that anyone who takes up this task and goes any distance at all with it will not be sorry.

Summary

To put aside the crutch of relying on a tarot manual and take your readings and your psychic abilities to the next level in which you can perform phenomenal readings with detailed accuracy, you must master the following main components of esoteric science:

1. The 22 letters of the Hebrew alphabet and their meanings, which are embodied in the major arcana.

2. The astrological symbols of the planets and the zodiac and their meanings, which are embodied in the numbered cards of the minor arcana.

3. The four elements and the combinations of these elements, which are embodied in the aces and the court cards.

If you master these things and apply them, you will soon be able to perform marvelous feats with the tarot cards, especially Crowley's *Thoth* deck.

HOW TO ADVANCE YOUR PSYCHIC ABILITIES

When you perform your first tarot readings, you are still learning the basic meanings of the cards in their various positions, trying to master the technical aspects of conducting a reading and beginning to develop a personal style. But, once you have truly mastered the meanings of the cards and other aspects of giving readings your psychic abilities begin unfolding very rapidly.

As discussed in the previous chapter, the *Thoth* deck is possibly the most meaningfully illustrated of any that are available and studying the symbolism in the deck can forever free you from mechanical readings and the use of tarot manuals.

To take your readings to the ultimate level and open the door to advanced psychic abilities, it is important to have the initiation into the occult mysteries of the tarot provided by a close study of the symbolism in this deck.

This next level of tarot mastery can be likened to learning how to drive a car. In the beginning, you have to apply a lot of thought and attention to the mechanical aspects of the gears, the gas pedal, the brakes and steering. But, after you have mastered those aspects of this skill, you are able to drive without conscious attention to these things.

Similarly, after you get past the mechanics of tarot reading and make an in-depth study of the cards and their symbolism becomes very familiar to you, then you can begin to rely more on your intuitive ability, which now has a foundation in an understanding of the esoteric mysteries of the cards.

How an Advanced Tarot Reader Conducts a Reading

When a querent comes to you, ask them not to provide you with any information about themselves. As an advanced reader, you should not need to make use of crutches you might have used in your first readings, such as asking the querent's birth date. Any details the querent gives you about themselves could prejudice your readings.

Sometimes a querent will state the purpose of their visit before you have a chance to stop them, but it is always better if they do not. You should be able to identify the situation and the surrounding questions, which have brought them to you, once you lay out the cards. If they begin to tell you the purpose of their visit, gently interrupt them and say, "Please, don't tell me anymore. It's part of my job to tell you why you're here."

Then, seat the querent across from you at your card table. Quickly go into trance, lay the cards and begin the reading.

Tell the querent the situation at hand and the purpose of their visit as you see it in the cards. Ask if this is correct, because if it is not, you do not want to continue on that course with your reading. At this point, the querent will probably clarify the purpose of their visit; if not, you can ask.

When you are at this level of mastery with your readings, you should be able to look at the tableau and discern the reason for the querent's visit in a matter of seconds. You will probably never be able to tell the querent the reason for their visit correctly every time, but you should work to get it right 80 to 90 percent of the time. One reason for getting it wrong can be that there are factors at work in the querent's life that you can see, which he or she is not yet aware of.

During the course of the reading, look carefully at the symbolism and the artwork in the cards. If one or more details particularly draw your attention, focus on that for a moment, then listen and look within for any messages. Focus on whatever attracts your attention most and trust the signals you receive. Convey the messages you receive to the querent and confirm whether they are valid or not.

By using this method, you will be able to entertain and amaze your clients while serving a much higher purpose as a medium and psychic advisor.

How to Let Go of Your Biased Judgments

It is natural to make judgments about people. It is a fact of life that we judge each other all the time. Usually, we do it subconsciously and it is not something easily shut off. For example, some people may assume that a man with long hair is a hippie, a biker or a musician or they may assume that someone who wears glasses is really smart. They may be tempted to project their own desires or preferences on others because of the biases they hold. When you monitor your thoughts, you will likely find yourself making similar judgments.

When you become aware that you are doing this with a querent, acknowledge it. Then, the instant you sit down across from them, put these judgments aside. Most of the time, such spontaneous judgments will be completely wrong and if you allow yourself to hold onto them, it could prejudice you and cause you to give an inaccurate reading.

So, when you first see your client, be aware of your superficial judgments. Once you begin to lay the cards, get in the habit of releasing those initial impressions and their accompanying biases so that you can accept what the cards are telling you without the interference of personal biases. When the cards begin to tell you things that are completely contrary to your first impressions of the querent, this is another way to know you are in the zone. You know that this information is coming from another source besides yourself because it is either contrary to your own thoughts or completely unrelated to them. Confirm the messages you are receiving with your querent.

Eventually, you won't really need to ask because the cards will tell you and you will simply know when you are right. Still, confirm your impressions with the querent because while you are developing your abilities, you must take care of your client. Always consider his or her own preferences and feelings and do not invalidate them by denying them or imposing your ideas on them.

You will soon find that it is easier to read for complete strangers than people you know even a little bit. This is because once you know anything at all about a person, your mind will naturally latch onto those facts and your biases regarding that information will obstruct your ability to give a true psychic reading.

Going from Tarot Reader to Psychic: Clairvoyance and Clairaudience

As you conduct your tarot readings, focus on balancing your analysis of the cards with looking and listening inwardly.

As you do this, you may spontaneously begin experiencing clairvoyance, which is literally "second sight," in which you receive and interpret visual signals by means of something other than your physical eyes. When you mentally see things you do not recognize as your own memories or your own thoughts, they are probably related to your querent.

You may, also, experience clairaudience, which is receiving a message by means of a sound. When it is not your own internal monologue – that voice that you use in your own mind that says things like, "Darn it! I forgot my keys!" – then you know that it is coming from somewhere else.

I often have a sense that my mental field has merged with that of the querent and I am pulling pictures or sounds of his or her mind. Although, at other times, these signals seem to come from a different source. In my own experience these pictures and sounds are not produced in my mind. I see or hear them as if they were projected out into near space. In my case, images appear to my upper left, somewhat as if they are being projected onto a screen, but the quality of the vision is three-dimensional. I've learned that this is a cue that I am having a psychic experience and I regularly test the accuracy of this information by confirming facts obtained this way with my clients.

When there is a sensation that my mental field has merged with theirs and a silent rapport has been established, this is when the readings are often the easiest to perform, the information comes quickly, very clearly and it is dead eye accurate. Your goal as a psychic reader of the tarot card is to attain this kind of easy psychic rapport.

Again, always confirm your impressions with the querent to gauge your accuracy. After you read the tarot cards this way for a while, this sense of knowing, which is a gnosis or inner knowing, will expand to other areas of your life outside of tarot card reading. Your psychic abilities will increase dramatically and remain that way all the time, not just during readings.

Spiritual Aide

Requesting and receiving spiritual assistance can dramatically improve the quality of your readings and expand your psychic abilities. One simple and unobtrusive method you can use to improve your readings is simply to silently ask for help from a deity, angels or any good spirits who take an interest in your querent's life. Before you lay the cards, silently ask, "Is there anyone here who can help this person?" Often you will have the sense of presences in the room with you who may be able to provide you with information that can help the querent.

Some people assume without question that there are spirits around us, whether the spirits of deceased family members or angelic beings. For other people, this is more difficult to believe. When you have experiences of your own that help you to verify the existence of such things, it is easier for the rational mind to accept.

As you progress in the development of your skills, do what you are comfortable with. Do not be limited by your belief or lack thereof, but approach it as an experiment without any expectations. Beliefs can become obstacles. Let your experiences, rather than your beliefs, guide you. Always be prepared to cast aside your current view of the world in light of new information. Often, the world is not as we believe it to be.

Separating Your Thoughts from the Querent's

When your psychic abilities first begin to expand, it is often a challenge to find the boundaries between your own mental activity and someone else's. While you are performing a reading, you may have thoughts, images, information, and emotions coming into your mind, which may or may not be your own. They may be easily confused with your own inner monologue or memories. You must determine which of these thoughts and emotions are really yours and which are coming from the querent or some other source.

To maintain a psychic boundary between yourself and the querent, it is imperative that you remove yourself from your own problems at the time of the reading. A technique I use when I sit with a client is to tell myself, "This is my job right now. I will go back to worrying about my own problems only after this reading is finished."

It is important to recognize the particular way you feel when you prove to yourself that you are actually completely focusing on your querent and getting information that is coming from a source outside yourself. It is difficult to explain exactly how to distinguish yourself from the person you are reading for, but, you will know when you have done it. When your advanced psychic abilities begin to unfold, it is important for you reaffirm the information you obtain by psychic means. Confirming your impressions with the querent helps you find the boundary between the signals of your own mental activity and those of someone else's.

Once you have located this boundary, you will learn to recognize it nearly every time. It is a distinctive sensation and something that can only be accomplished with careful self-monitoring and verifying the experience with the people you read for. After a while you will just know things about people, your surroundings and future events by your psychic abilities without using the cards. This is why, when properly employed, the tarot cards are a very powerful tool for psychic development.

As your abilities continue to unfold, you will become more confident and you will amaze your clients because you will be able to sit with complete strangers and tell them things about themselves that they have never told anyone.

APPENDIX

Herbs, Foods, Minerals and Vitamins for Optimizing Psychic Abilities

General Warning: Consult your doctor before adding any herbs, foods, minerals, vitamins or other supplements to your diet. Take special caution if you are pregnant, nursing or under the care of a physician for any condition. Some herbs have natural abortificant powers when consumed as teas and tinctures and this is noted wherever possible, however, some herbs which are not generally considered dangerous or toxic can still present a danger to some people. For example, there are some people who are allergic to the entire mint family, which is generally considered safe. Use common sense and whenever you are in doubt about the safety of an herb, mineral, vitamin or other supplement, consult a qualified physician.

Herbs and Foods

Acai berries: Lucid dreams; prophesy and clairvoyance

Anise, Mediterranean (Pimpinella anisum): Improves psychic abilities

Anise, Star (Illicium verum): Divination; clarity and focus

Apple cider vinegar (raw with the mother): Tonic for the entire body; natural pH balancer

Bay leaf: Clairvoyance; visions

Bearberry (Uva ursi): Psychic enhancement and meditation

Berries, dark red and blue: Enhanced physical and metaphysical vision; vivid dreams

Bing cherries: (see recipe for jelly below)

Bladderwrack: Clairvoyance

Bleeding Heart (Dicentra formosa): Divination **(Warning:** Do not take internally if pregnant, nursing or if you have a liver condition.)

Borage: Psychic development

Bracken: Divination

Bromeliad (Crypanthus): Divination

Calendula: Psychic development

Camphor: Divination; spiritual cleansing; healing and past lives

Carrots: A natural source of rhodium and beta carotene; liver detoxifier; improves physical and metaphysical vision

Celery seed: Deep concentration and focus

Chicory: Psychic enhancement

Chocolate, raw: To connect with spirits; an ancient offering to the spirits in Latin America

Chlorella: Mercury chelator for a healthy nervous system

Cinnamon: Increases personal vibratory rate; enhances the ability to receive spirit communication

Citron (Citrus medica): Psychic abilities

Clary Sage: Visions; divination

Cloves: Divination

Club moss: Divination

Concord grapes: A natural source of iridium; increases the personal vibratory rate and enhances psychic abilities

Dandelion: Liver and blood tonic; psychic dreams and divination

Elderberry: Visions

Essiac Tea (Guardian Spirit Tea): A reputed anti-cancer tea blend that includes burdock root, sheep sorrel, slippery elm and Turkey rhubarb and is a natural source of iridium; increases the personal vibratory rate and enhances psychic abilities

Eyebright: Enhances physical and metaphysical vision

Flax seed (crushed or oil): Healthy brain tissue; psychic development

Garlic: Clairvoyance

Ginger: A natural source of melatonin, a hormone secreted by the pineal gland

Hibiscus: Lust; love and divination

Honeysuckle: Divination

Hops: Relaxed focus; sleep and divination

Kale: High in beta carotene

Lemongrass: Relaxant; enhances focus and psychic abilities

Lettuce: Divination and protection from ghosts

Mandrake (European): Love; wealth; protection; effigy magic and divination. (Poison. Do not ingest)

Marjoram: Psychic development

Mugwort: Increased awareness; use in sachets and sparingly as a tea (Warning: Abortificant; Do not ingest if pregnant or nursing.)

Parsley: A nervine; keeps the nervous system in optimal working condition

Peppermint: Sharpens the senses

Rosemary: Spirit communication

Sweet potatoes: Source of beta carotene

Tamarind: Pineal gland detoxifier

Valerian root: Anti-anxiety herb; enhances focus and relaxation

Wheatgrass: Natural source of chlorella; a detoxifier

Wormwood: Dreams; visions; psychic enhancement

Yerba santera: Clairvoyance and clairaudience

Use the following as incense:

Acacia: Visions of the dead

Amber or Ambergris: To open the third eye

Copal: To summon spirits

Elecampane: Psychic development

Frankincense: Enhanced concentration and focus; visions

Myrrh: To summon spirits

Sandalwood: To open the third eye

Tobacco: Spirit communication

Herbal Tea for Relaxation, Enhanced Focus and Psychic Abilities

1 to 1 1/2 cups boiling water
1 tsp. Ginger
Pinch of Lemongrass
1 tsp. Valerian root, crushed or 1/2" long piece of whole root

Allow this mixture to cool, strain it and add honey or sugar to taste. Drink this tea before bedtime.

Tips and Tricks to Enhance Psychic Abilities

Enhance your overall psychic abilities by drinking a little tea made of mugwort and raw chicory. Alternatively, placing a little muslin bag of mugwort under your pillow may enhance your psychic abilities.

Tiger's eye, lapis lazuli and amber are helpful stones for opening the third eye. Wear jewelry made of these stones close to the skin. Alternatively, make gem elixirs by putting the clean stones into a jug of distilled water and leaving it in the refrigerator overnight. Then, remove the stones and drink the water.

Apply ambergris (amber essential oil) to the third eye, chakra right between your eyebrows to stimulate your sixth sense.

Candle Spell for Psychic Enhancement

On the night of a full moon, preferably on a Monday or a Thursday, anoint a dark blue candle with essential oil of ambergris, frankincense or sandalwood while repeating, "By the power of three times three, bring the psychic enhancement to me." In a safe place, light the candle, meditate on the flame and let it burn down. Bury the remains in your front yard. Perform this spell more than once, if necessary.

Minerals

Boron: A necessary trace mineral for all tissues; many people are deficient

Chromium: Necessary to make psychic connection

Copper: A balance is necessary for psychic abilities

Iodine (Heritage Products' Sea-Adine or Lugol's drops): Combats the effects of radiation on the glands and fortifies the pineal gland (third eye chakra) against common toxins

Iridium: A trace mineral that enhances psychic abilities

Rhodium: A trace mineral that enhances psychic abilities

Selenium: Necessary to make psychic connection

Vitamins

Vitamin A and its precursor Beta carotene: Necessary for physical and metaphysical vision

Vitamin C: Oxygenation and energy

Vitamins K1 & K2: Pineal gland activators

Nostradamus' Recipe for Cherry Jelly

The following is based on Nostradamus' original recipe, which was written in French. An English translation is given in an article entitled, "Nostradmus Cherry Jelly," at *FXcyuisine.com.* [4] It is taken from the book, *EXCELLENT & USEFUL Treatise to all Needed Who Want Knowledge of Several Exquisite Recipes ... Newly Composed by Master Michel de Nostredame, Doctor of Medicine in the City of Salon de Craux en Provence*, published in 1555.

According to Nostradamus, these recipes were written to satisfy those who wish to know and understand new things.

Equipment:

Large pot, approximately 16 to 20 quarts
Large spoon
Large ladle
Ball or Mason jars with sealable lids
Jar grabber
Jelly strainer or clean gauze
Funnel

Ingredients:

6 to 7 pounds stemmed Bing cherries
1 to 2 pounds coarse sugar

Note: The original recipe does not call for pectin, so this jelly may be thinner, more like a syrup. If the taste is too sweet, add one or two teaspoons of lemon juice. A few drops of lemon juice may, also, be added as a preservative.

Instructions:

Wash and stem the cherries. In a large pot, boil the cherries until they are reduced by half. Reduce heat and simmer for 10 minutes. Strain the juice. Add sugar. Boil for, at least, one minute or until the juice congeals when dropped upon a cool surface like a slab of marble or a piece of tin. Then, remove the pot from the heat and skim off the foam.

Scald the jars and lids. Ladle the liquid into jars leaving 1/4 inch space at the top. Screw the lids down tightly.

REFERENCES

1."Police Arrest Fortune Tellers," *Associated Press, The Spokesman-Review and Spokane Chronicle,* Monday, January 18, 1991, Spokane, Washington, P. 10. http://news.google.com/newspapers? nid=1314&dat=19910128&id=muRPAAAAIBAJ& sjid=YggEAAAAIBAJ&pg=4978,4211839

2. "Fortune Tellers Couldn't Predict Their Own Future," *Associated Press,* The Free Lance-Star, Fredericksburg, Viginia, Friday, February 8, 1991, P. 22. http://news.google.com/newspapers? nid=1298&dat=19910208&id=SXQQAAAAIBAJ &sjid=X4sDAAAAIBAJ&pg=6977,1224692

3. Sehgal, Renu, "Fortunetellers and Psychics Battle Connecticut Ban as Rights Violation," Associated Press, Los Angeles Times, November 29, 1992 http://articles.latimes.com/1992-11-29/news/mn-2758_1_psychic-fair

4. Nostradmus Cherry Jelly," *FXcyuisine.com*
(http://fxcuisine.com/Default.asp?
language=2&Display=200&resolution=high

MORE WINTER TEMPEST BOOKS

If you enjoyed this book, you might enjoy other Winter Tempest Books:

All Natural Dental Remedies: Herbs and Home Remedies to Heal Your Teeth & Naturally Restore Tooth Enamel by Angela Kaelin

Black Magic for Dark Times: Spells of Revenge and Protection by Angela Kaelin

Blood and Black Roses: A Dark Bouquet of Vampires, Romance and Horror by Sophia diGregorio (Fiction)

The Forgotten: The Vampire Prince by Sophia diGregorio (Fiction)

How to Communicate with Spirits: Séances, Ouija Boards and Summoning by Angela Kaelin

How to Develop Advanced Psychic Abilities: Obtain Information about the Past, Present and Future Through Clairvoyance by Sophia diGregorio

Grimoire of Santa Muerte: Spells and Rituals of Most Holy Death, the Unofficial Saint of Mexico by Sophia diGregorio

How to Write Your Own Spells for Any Purpose and Make Them Work by Sophia diGregorio

Magical Healing: How to Use Your Mind to Heal Yourself and Others by Angela Kaelin

Natural Remedies for Reversing Gray Hair: Nutrition and Herbs for Anti-aging and Optimum Health by Thomas W. Xander

Practical Black Magic: How to Hex and Curse Your Enemies by Sophia diGregorio

Spells for Money and Wealth by Angela Kaelin

To Conjure the Perfect Man by Sophia diGregorio (Fiction)

The Traditional Witches' Book of Love Spells by Angela Kaelin

Traditional Witches' Formulary and Potion-making Guide: Recipes for Magical Oils, Powders and Other Potions by Sophia diGregorio

ABOUT THE AUTHOR

Angela Kaelin is the author of metaphysical books, such as, *How to Communicate with Spirits: Séances, Ouija Boards and Summoning, The Traditional Witches' Book of Love Spells, Spells for Money and Wealth,* and *Magical Healing: How to Use Your Mind to Heal Yourself and Others.* She is, also, an alternative health writer and the author of *All Natural Dental Remedies: Herbs and Home Remedies to Heal Your Teeth & Naturally Restore Tooth Enamel.*

Disclaimer: The author and publisher of this guide has used her best efforts in preparing this document. The author makes no representation or warranties with respect to the accuracy, applicability, fitness or completeness of the contents of this document. The author disclaims any warranties expressed or implied. The author of this book is not a medical or legal professional and is not qualified to give medical or legal advice. Nothing in this document should be construed as medical or legal advice. The material in this book is presented for informational purposes only. The procedures described in this book should not be used a substitute for treatment from state approved, licensed medical authorities.

Nothing in this book should be construed as incitement to dangerous or illegal acts and the reader is advised to be aware of and heed all pertinent laws in his or her city, state, country or other jurisdiction. Any medical or legal questions should be addressed to the proper medical or legal authorities. The author shall in no event be held liable for any losses or damages, including but not limited to special, incidental, consequential or other damages incurred by the use of this information. Always take proper precautions with candles, sharp objects, essential oils, herbs and use only as directed.

The statements in this book have not been evaluated by any other government entity. The statements contained herein represent the legally protected opinions of the author and are presented for informational purposes only. Anyone who uses any of the information in the book does so at their own risk with the understanding that the author cannot be held responsible for the consequences.

FTC Disclaimer: The author has no connection to nor was paid by any brand or product described in this document with the exception of any other books mentioned which were written by the author or published by Winter Tempest Books.